STAGE 3

FANTASTIC
AND
STRANGE

**BY BEN HULME-CROSS
AND PAUL STEWART**

**ILLUSTRATED BY ALESSANDRO VALDRIGHI,
CARLO MOLINARI, CATHERINE PEARSON,
PATRICK MILLER, DANIELA TERRAZZINI AND
EUAN COOK**

OXFORD
UNIVERSITY PRESS

CONTENTS

THE HOUND OF THE BASKERVILLES

BY SIR ARTHUR CONAN DOYLE
RETOLD BY BEN HULME-CROSS
ILLUSTRATED BY ALESSANDRO VALDRIGHI

Setting the scene

Have you heard of Sherlock Holmes, the famous detective? He is a character first created by the author Sir Arthur Conan Doyle in a series of stories written about a hundred years ago and still popular today. He is well known for being incredibly clever and able to solve mysterious crimes – but also for being extremely rude! The story you are about to read is told by Sherlock's assistant, Doctor Watson.

Of all the cases brought to the door of Sherlock Holmes, the mystery of the hound of the Baskervilles was perhaps the most memorable.

Old Sir Charles Baskerville was dead, and Holmes suspected murder. The old man's son and heir, Henry Baskerville, had returned to Baskerville Hall from overseas, and now he was receiving threatening letters. Baskerville Hall was isolated, high on the moors, with only one near neighbour, Jack Stapleton.

To add to the mystery, there was even a family curse. Legend had it that centuries before, another Baskerville, Sir Hugo, committed a terrible crime on the moors and was then devoured by a huge, glowing hound that had plagued the family ever since.

Sherlock Holmes was a most infuriating man. Even I, his closest ally, was never told the details of his plans until he revealed them in one of his grand crime-solving performances. So it was, that awful night on the moor as we lay in wait.

"Why do you think Jack Stapleton murdered Sir Charles?" I hissed. "And why would he want to kill Henry Baskerville? Even if he does intend to kill him, why go to the trouble of doing it out here on the moor?"

"Perfectly simple, my dear Watson," replied Holmes, never looking at me once. "I suspect Stapleton because I believe he is a descendent of Sir Hugo Baskerville. He bears a striking resemblance to a portrait of Sir Hugo at Baskerville Hall. And he won't kill Henry in his own house because he wants it to look like an accident."

A thick layer of fog was rolling towards us, creeping silently across the moor. I shivered, unable to banish from my mind thoughts of the Baskerville family curse.

"So the threats Henry has received ..."

"Sent by Stapleton, I am sure of it," said Holmes curtly. "Designed to frighten Henry. Stapleton wants to get rid of Henry and inherit Baskerville Hall. 'The family curse is upon you,' he says. 'Beware the hound on the moors.' Really! Come now, my dear chap. You're a man of science! You don't believe in curses or mysterious hounds, do you, Dr Watson?"

"But what about the howls we have heard coming from the moor? And the footprints we have seen?"

"The howls and footprints were designed to frighten Henry still further."

I blinked and shook my head. Holmes was right. There had to be a rational explanation. Glowing hounds did not roam the moors at night, devouring members of the English gentry!

Yet tales of curses and monstrous beasts, on a night like that one, had a certain power ...

All of a sudden, Holmes pressed an ear to the ground. "Footsteps!" he muttered. "Henry is coming."

The moon still shone bright, but the wall of fog was closing in on us fast. I could hear the footsteps myself now – a man running hard. Behind the footsteps, another sound carried through the fog. It was a thin, crisp, continuous patter.

Nothing more terrible could ever be imagined than the beast which followed Henry out of the wall of fog. It was an enormous, coal-black hound. Fire burst from its open mouth. Its eyes glowed. Its jaws and head and shoulders shone with luminous flame.

The huge black creature was leaping down the track, following hard after Henry. I looked at Holmes.

For the briefest of moments, he seemed too stunned to act, but then he reached into his coat and pulled out a tube the size of a small flute which he brought to his lips. A blowgun!

A dart shot from the tube and the creature gave a hideous howl. It did not pause, however, but bounded on. In front of us, as we raced up the track, we heard scream after scream from Henry and the deep roar of the hound.

We reached them just as the beast sprang and hurled Henry to the ground. It seemed poised to bite Henry's neck, when it staggered suddenly. It gave a plaintive howl, snapped its jaws at the air, and then fell limp on its side. The giant hound was unconscious. Holmes's dart had been drugged.

I ran my hand over the hound's glowing head and my palm came away glowing too.

"He's been painted with phosphorus to make him glow!" I said. "It's make-up! The kind of trick you might see on stage!"

The terrible hound of the Baskervilles was just a big bloodhound that had been made to look monstrous and set to chase Henry.

"This was Stapleton's work!" Holmes exclaimed.

Suddenly, we heard a faint cry from across the moor.

"Save me! Somebody save me! I'm sinking in the bog!"

It was Stapleton's voice, of that I was sure. Yet though we searched, we never did find him.

Henry returned home to Baskerville Hall, but never received another threatening letter.

The Mystery of the Mary Celeste

BY BEN-HULME CROSS

ILLUSTRATED BY CARLO MOLINARI

Setting the scene

In this text, you are going to be the detective in a real-life mystery. You will read the facts about an event that genuinely took place in the year 1872. Over the years, many people have tried to solve the mystery and you will read some of the explanations that have been suggested. However, to this day, no one really knows the answers ... so now it's your turn to investigate the mystery of the *Mary Celeste*.

The Mystery of the Mary Celeste

Sir Arthur Conan Doyle, the author of the Sherlock Holmes stories, liked a good real-life mystery. He wrote a fictional account based on the true story of the ship, the *Mary Celeste*, which became very popular. But what really happened to the mysterious *Mary Celeste*?

On 7th November 1872, Captain Benjamin Briggs and his experienced crew set sail from New York in the *Mary Celeste*. They were taking a cargo of around 1700 barrels across the Atlantic to Genoa in Italy.

Captain Briggs was expecting a straight-forward voyage, and he was pleased that his wife and two-year-old daughter were coming with him.

Meanwhile, just up the coast, Captain David Morehouse was also making ready to sail to Genoa. His ship, the *Dei Gratia*, set sail eight days after the *Mary Celeste* and followed roughly the same course.

Captain Benjamin Briggs

On 5th December, in the middle of the Atlantic, the crew of the *Dei Gratia* saw a ship sailing erratically in their direction. Unable to see anyone on deck, Captain Morehouse sent two of his men to investigate.

They realized that it was the *Mary Celeste* and climbed aboard, where they discovered that the ship had been abandoned.

Where had the captain and crew disappeared to, and why?

Some of the sails were rolled up, though some of them were torn, and there were ropes hanging over the sides of the ship and trailing in the water. There was some water below deck in the hold, but not a dangerous amount.

The barrels were still in the hold, and plenty of food and water was still stashed away tidily in the ship's galley. The lifeboat was missing, as was some of the captain's navigational equipment.

There was no sign of a struggle or a fire, and the last entry in the ship's log had been written ten days previously, on 25th November, when the *Mary Celeste* had been 400 miles away

Captain Morehouse hoped for a big reward for the recovery of the *Mary Celeste*. He split his crew of eight in two, and sailed both the *Mary Celeste* and the *Dei Gratia* safely into harbour at Gibraltar.

Possible explanations

Here are just some of the many different theories explaining what might have happened to the *Mary Celeste*. Give each theory marks out of five, to show how believable you think it is.

Piracy ☆☆☆☆☆

Some people think that pirates attacked the *Mary Celeste* and carried off the captain, his wife and daughter, and the crew.

However, would pirates do all this without stealing the ship's cargo? Pirates are in the business of stealing things to make themselves rich, so this theory seems unlikely.

Mutiny ☆☆☆☆☆

Others have suggested that the crew of the *Mary Celeste* rose up in mutiny against Captain Briggs. The problem with this theory is that Briggs was a well-respected captain and the crew were all reliable men. What's more, if there had been a mutiny, why would everyone have abandoned ship?

Waterspout ☆☆☆☆☆

Some historians have suggested that the *Mary Celeste* may have encountered a waterspout – a tornado over the sea that causes a tube of water to rise up into the air.

This does sound possible. Perhaps the captain and crew feared they were in danger of sinking, and fled in the lifeboat for that reason.

However, others have argued that if there was a waterspout, nobody would choose to take their chances in a lifeboat instead of staying on-board a sturdy ship.

Running aground ☆☆☆☆☆

If he thought the ship was going to run on to rocks, the captain may have ordered everyone into the lifeboat. This might have sunk, while the wind picked up and blew the *Mary Celeste* clear of the rocks.

However, if this had happened, the crew would have been using every sail as they tried to avoid the rocks; but the *Mary Celeste* was found with many sails rolled up.

Fraud ☆☆☆☆☆

Was it all an elaborate performance – a hoax?

On the one hand, Captain Morehouse and Captain Briggs could well have been friends. They might have planned for Morehouse to recover the 'lost' ship, and then split the reward with Briggs.

On the other hand, Captain Morehouse would have needed brilliant acting skills to get away with this. Also, Captain Briggs left behind a son who was unable to come on the voyage. Would he really have abandoned his son?

So, which of these theories do you think is the most likely? Or can you think of any other explanations yourself?

MACAVITY:
THE MYSTERY CAT

BY T.S. ELIOT

ILLUSTRATED BY CATHERINE PEARSON

Setting the scene

T.S. Eliot is one of the most famous poets of the 20th Century and some of his poems can be quite challenging to understand. However, he was also very fond of cats and he wrote a series of poems about different types of cats to entertain some children that he knew. Here is one of those poems for you to read and enjoy. (Tip: it is even better if you read it out loud.)

MACAVITY:
THE MYSTERY CAT

This famous poem by T.S. Eliot is about a cat who's a master criminal. Although he's never actually spotted at the scene, Macavity is behind almost every crime you can imagine – and some you probably can't. It's quite a performance!

Macavity's a Mystery Cat: he's called the
Hidden Paw—

For he's the master criminal who can defy
the Law.

He's the bafflement of Scotland Yard, the
Flying Squad's despair:

For when they reach the scene of crime—
Macavity's not there!

Macavity, Macavity, there's no one like Macavity,

He's broken every human law, he breaks the law
of gravity.

His powers of **levitation** would make a
fakir stare,

And when you reach the scene of crime—
Macavity's not there!

You may seek him in the basement, you may
look up in the air—

But I tell you once and once again, *Macavity's
not there!*

levitation	floating in the air
fakir	a man who works wonders

Macavity's a ginger cat, he's very tall and thin;

You would know him if you saw him, for his
   eyes are sunken in.

His brow is deeply lined with thought, his head
   is highly domed;

His coat is dusty from neglect, his whiskers
   are uncombed.

He sways his head from side to side, with
   movements like a snake;

And when you think he's half asleep, he's
   always wide awake.

Macavity, Macavity, there's no one like Macavity,

For he's a fiend in **feline** shape, a monster
   of **depravity**.

You may meet him in a by-street, you may see him
   in the square—

But when a crime's discovered, then *Macavity's
   not there!*

| feline | cat-like |
| **depravity** | wickedness |

He's outwardly respectable. (They say he cheats
  at cards.)

And his footprints are not found in any file of
  Scotland Yard's

And when the **larder**'s looted, or the jewel-case
  is rifled,

Or when the milk is missing, or another **Peke**'s
  been stifled,

Or the greenhouse glass is broken, and the trellis
  past repair—

Ay, there's the wonder of the thing!
  Macavity's not there!

larder	a food cupboard
Peke	type of dog (Pekinese)
Treaty	important document

And when the Foreign Office find a **Treaty**'s
gone astray,

Or the Admiralty lose some plans and drawings
by the way,

There may be a scrap of paper in the hall or on
the stair—

But it's useless to investigate—*Macavity's
not there!*

And when the loss has been disclosed, the
Secret Service say:

'It *must* have been Macavity!'—but he's a
mile away.

You'll be sure to find him resting, or a-licking
of his thumbs;

Or engaged in doing complicated long
division sums.

Macavity, Macavity, there's no one like Macavity,

There never was a Cat of such deceitfulness and **suavity**.

He always has an **alibi**, and one or two to spare:

At whatever time the deed took place—
MACAVITY WASN'T THERE!

And they say that all the Cats whose wicked deeds are widely known

(I might mention Mungojerrie, I might mention Griddlebone)

Are nothing more than agents for the Cat who all the time

Just controls their operations: the Napoleon of Crime!

T.S. Eliot

suavity	sophistication
alibi	proof you were elsewhere when a crime was committed

THE HOWLER

BY PAUL STEWART
ILLUSTRATED BY PATRICK MILLER

Setting the scene

Imagine arriving at a place where no human has ever lived before, where there are no houses, shops or roads, no gas or electricity. Settlers are people who travel to new places and find ways to survive and build a new life. They live off the land, growing crops and hunting animals. They have to work together and protect each other from danger.

Chapter 1

"It's worse than I feared," said Jed Conway.

The leader of the Homestead was inspecting the damage caused by the previous night's storm. Stretches of the perimeter fence had blown down, half the houses had lost their roofs, and one of the main greenhouses had been destroyed – along with the precious fruit and vegetables growing inside it.

"We'll repair what we can while it's light," Jed told the others. "But we don't have much time."

"What about the clatter-traps?" asked Miller Groves. "Someone needs to see if we've got any animals trapped in them. Otherwise dinner will just be potatoes and cabbage. Again."

Jed shook his head. "I need everyone to help get those roofs fixed."

"I'll go," a voice piped up.

It was Brady Conway, Jed's son.

"No way," Amy Conway told him. "It's far too dangerous."

"Oh, but–" Brady began.

"I'll go with him," said Mac Wright.

Tall, powerfully-built and almost eighteen, Mac was Brady's cousin. A week earlier, he'd fallen from a ladder and broken his wrist. He raised a plastered arm. "Can't do much roof-mending with this."

Amy was still not happy for her young son to head into the forest, but in the end she agreed to let him go.

"Take care, Brady," she said. "And watch out for the howlers!"

*

"You ever seen a howler, Mac?" asked Brady.

"No," came the reply. "But I've heard them, and that's enough."

As if on cue, the sound of distant howling echoed through the air. Brady shuddered.

The two of them had set off from the Homestead an hour earlier, equipped with knives, forage-sacks and, for when night fell, torches made of wooden poles, their ends dipped in tar. The wind had dropped, but it was still freezing. Even here in the forest, the snow lay deep, and despite his thick socks and heavy boots Brady's feet ached with the cold.

40

"I don't reckon winter's ever going to end," he muttered miserably.

When the spaceship had first dropped the settlers on Planet 0733bx – or Styron as they named it – it had seemed ideal. The climate was gentle, the land fertile and there was plenty of wildlife to hunt. They built the Homestead, and started to farm the land.

Then everything changed.

Herds of animals that people depended on for food disappeared; birds gathered in flocks, took to the air and flew away, never to return. It grew darker, colder. Then the snow started to fall. Twelve years later, Styron was still in the grip of winter.

"It's because the planet's only got two seasons," said Mac. "Summer and winter – and each one of them lasts for decades." He sighed. "It was warm and sunny when I was little. I remember swimming in the river ..."

"Don't, Mac," said Brady.
He'd only ever known it like this:
blizzards, ice-storms. "Let's change the
subject. Where are those clatter-traps?"

"The first one's over there," said
Mac, pointing ahead to the base of a tall
tree. "But there's nothing in it."

When they got there, Brady looked at
the empty snare. "How did you know?"
he said.

Mac crouched down. "See here," he said.
"When an animal gets caught, these hanging
bits of metal come loose and clatter in the
wind. Like wind chimes. The noise frightens
off any scavengers. That's why they're called
clatter-traps," he added.

"So we just need to *listen* for them," said Brady, cocking his head to one side.

He couldn't hear any wind chimes, but the blood-curdling howls were getting closer.

*

The second trap they came to was also empty. So was the third, but Brady and Mac kept going. Everyone back at the Homestead was depending on them for dinner. The howling grew louder and when they came to a set of huge, clawed paw prints crossing their path, Mac stopped.

"We'd better light the torches," he said. "Just in case."

They trudged on through the icy forest, the flames from their torches flickering on the surrounding trees. Brady was beginning to lose hope, when suddenly, from up ahead, he heard the tell-tale sound of metal on metal. Moments later they came to a clatter-trap that *had* been tripped.

"A bouncer," said Mac, as he removed the dead hare-like creature from the snare and pushed it into his forage-sack. "And there's something else close by," he said. "Listen."

Following the sound, they headed still deeper into the forest. When they came to the second sprung clatter-trap, the first thing they saw was the circle of huge paw prints around the tree. Thankfully, the creature that had made them had not stolen the dead hoglet in the snare, but it might still be close.

"Stick it in your forage-sack," said Mac. "I'll keep guard."

Brady was doing what he was told when he heard Mac's sharp intake of breath. He spun round.

There, looming out of the darkness, was the biggest, most ferocious creature Brady had ever seen. The light from Mac's blazing torch gleamed on its bared teeth and savage claws. So *this* was a howler. Rooted to the spot, the two of them watched it raise its head – and the air around them filled with its long, loud, terrible howl.

"Now what?" Brady breathed.

THE HOWLER
Chapter 2

Chapter 2

The howler stared at the dead hoglet in Brady's shaking hands, drool dripping from the corners of its mouth. Then it looked up. Brady was struck by the intelligence that glowed in its unblinking yellow eyes. Suddenly, he knew what he had to do.

"Here," he murmured, and chucked the dead hoglet to the creature.

The howler seized the hoglet in its jaws, turned tail and ran off.

"What did you do that for?" Mac demanded furiously. "That was our dinner!"

"I know," said Brady. "But that creature – the howler – I don't think it meant us any harm. And it looked so ... so desperate."

Mac sighed. "Come on, you big softy," he said, and clapped Brady on the shoulder. "We'll just have to search a while longer."

Some time later, they came to another sprung clatter-trap and Brady pushed the bouncer it had snared into his forage-sack. Mac looked up at the sky.

"It's getting dark," he said. "We'd better head back."

Night came more quickly than either Brady or Mac expected. The temperature dropped, the wind moaned and snow started to fall. Soon, they were in the middle of a fierce blizzard. Their footprints disappeared beneath the fresh snow, and even with their blazing torches raised they could barely see ahead.

Numb with cold, Brady's fingers throbbed, his face felt like ice and his breath came in thick billowing clouds. Despite his thick gloves, fur-lined hat, thermal under-gear and padded trousers and jacket, the arctic conditions had seeped through his clothes and chilled him to the bone. He felt weak and hungry.

And very scared ...

Not that he was about to admit that to Mac. It was Brady's fault they were in this situation and he was trying hard to be brave, but his fear must have shown in his face.

"We're gonna be fine, Brady," Mac told him. "Trust me."

Brady nodded. He did trust Mac. His older cousin had always supported him, looked out for him. But what if they got lost? Since winter had come to Styron, no one from the Homestead had ever survived a night out in the forest. As the sky turned pitch black, and the torches burned down, and the snow grew thicker, and the cold bit into him as painfully as any howler's fangs, Brady's fears grew.

Then an ear-splitting howl pierced the night.
"Mac!" Brady screamed.

The howler was back. It loomed up in front
of them. Huge and fearsome, its jaws were
slavering and its eyes glinted in the torchlight.

Mac and Brady both waved the dwindling
flames of their torches at it. The creature did not
retreat – but nor did it attack. Instead, it slowly
turned, walked off three paces, then looked back
at them. Then it did the same again, and again.

"I think it wants us to follow it," said Brady.

Mac snorted. "Leading us into a trap, most likely," he said.

"I don't think so," said Brady. "If it had wanted to eat the bouncers – or us – it would have attacked by now. It's big and mean enough."

Mac didn't say anything. But when the howler looked back a fourth time, he took Brady by the arm and the two of them followed it.

They walked through the dark forest in silence, with the howler just ahead, still checking every so often that they were keeping up. Brady was beginning to wonder whether this *was* a trap after all, when they arrived at one of the clatter-traps they'd emptied earlier.

Moments later, and without any warning, the howler abruptly bounded ahead and disappeared. Far in the distance, Brady and Mac saw the lights of the Homestead twinkling between the trees.

*

"It's true," Brady insisted, as everyone tucked into their meaty stew. "The creature led us all the way back here."

Mac was nodding. "It saved our lives," he told them.

No one believed their story though. It was simply too incredible.

"Pull the other one," Jed Conway said, and laughed. "I don't think–"

His words were interrupted by the sound of loud howling. This time, it wasn't just one creature, but several.

55

Leaving their half-eaten meals, the settlers all jumped up and dashed outside. They crossed the yard to the gate in the newly mended perimeter fence and looked out. There, standing in a line at the edge of the forest, was a family of howlers – father, mother and four cubs – each one with its head raised, howling at the sky.

When the people appeared, they fell silent. The father howler looked at Brady, who stared back, smiling. Then, without a sound, all six of them turned and trotted back into the trees.

"One good turn deserves another, eh?" said Jed Conway. "Well done, Brady. I'm proud of you, son."

Polar Exploration
SHOULD PEOPLE DO IT?

BY PAUL STEWART
ILLUSTRATED BY SCOTT JESSOP

Setting the scene

The polar regions, the Arctic and Antarctic, are among the most extreme environments on Earth. They are freezing, icy wildernesses where it is incredibly hard for humans to survive. What makes people want to go there – and should they be allowed to? The information in this text will help you make up your own mind about the answer to these questions.

Polar Exploration

SHOULD PEOPLE DO IT?

The Arctic and Antarctic are cold, inhospitable and dangerous landscapes. Most people feel no need to experience them for themselves. However, some explorers cannot resist the challenge offered by such remote and hostile environments.

Arctic

Antarctic

Reaching the poles

In the early 20th Century, several attempts were made to reach the poles. Robert Peary and Frederick Cook both claimed to be the first person to reach the North Pole, while in Antarctica, the Norwegian explorer Roald Amundsen beat Robert Falcon Scott and Ernest Shackleton to the South Pole.

Roald Amundsen reaches the South Pole

Although both poles have now been conquered, people continue to want to reach them. In 1993 Ann Bancroft became the first woman to reach both poles, while in 2017 Ernest Shackleton's great-grandson was part of a team that drove a passenger car across Antarctica for the first time. However, such expeditions are perilous and not always successful, like Sir Ranulph Fiennes's 'Coldest Journey' expedition of 2012.

The Coldest Journey

Sir Ranulph Fiennes and his team of five explorers aimed to be the first to cross the Antarctic in winter. Their journey would be over 3000 kilometres long, travelling in near total darkness, in temperatures as low as -90°C, five times colder than a kitchen freezer! They took enough food and equipment to last thirteen months, as no rescue or re-supply teams would be able to reach them.

Unfortunately, Fiennes had to pull out after he got frostbite while training. The others went ahead in early 2013 but had to stop after about 300 kilometres as extreme weather made it too dangerous to continue. They stayed to do important scientific research, returning home in November 2013.

The planned route

START
CROWN BAY

• PRINCESS
ELIZABETH
STATION

• AMUNDSEN-SCOTT
SOUTH POLE STATION

ROSS ISLAND
FINISH

Opinions about polar exploration

Public attitudes to such expeditions vary widely. Some people claim that adventures like these are irresponsible, while others argue that it is in the nature of human beings to push themselves to the limit. Every mountain must be climbed, every ocean must be dived, every desert must be crossed. Why? The answer is often: "Because it is there!"

Those who argue against polar exploration point out that if an expedition goes wrong and rescue teams have to be called out, this endangers the rescuers' lives. However, Ranulph Fiennes and his team decided not to ask for help, no matter what happened. Although this sounds admirable, it does not take into account families and friends at home who suffer tremendous stress worrying about their loved ones.

Is polar exploration too expensive?

Critics of polar exploration often think that it is a waste of money. They believe that while many people in the world live in extreme poverty, it is immoral for so much to be spent on a single expedition. Supporters say that the money is largely raised by public appeals for voluntary funding, as well as by business sponsors, who donate clothes and equipment so that their products can be advertised.

In addition, these supporters also point out that expeditions can raise money for charities. For example, Fiennes's expeditions have raised over £18 million for charity, and he has been named the UK's top celebrity fundraiser.

Charity logo

Advancing scientific knowledge

Another argument made by opponents is that polar exploration serves no useful purpose. "What is the point of skiing across Antarctica?" they ask. In answer, supporters stress that such expeditions enable important scientific studies to be carried out. The 'Coldest Journey' team did research to help scientists understand the effects of climate change upon the poles.

Furthermore, supporters point out that such information forms the basis of education programmes that reach hundreds of thousands of children in schools around the globe: children who will grow up to be the scientists, engineers and leaders of tomorrow.

Impact on the environment

When Cook and Amundsen set off on polar expeditions last century, their understanding of the world around them was quite different from ours today. Back then, they killed seals and penguins in order to survive, and made no attempt to be careful about their impact on the environment.

In contrast, Fiennes's team took all their food with them and left nothing behind which might upset the delicate balance of the polar wilderness. Despite this, many experts remain concerned that wherever human beings go, they affect the environment negatively.

Arguments FOR

In favour of polar exploration:
- humans should be free to push themselves to the limit;
- raises money for charities;
- enables scientific study;
- increases our knowledge of the world.

...and AGAINST

Against polar exploration:
▶ endangers lives of rescuers;
▶ effect on family and friends at home;
▶ too expensive – money could be spent elsewhere;
▶ impact on environment.

Abandoned tractor in Antarctica

Thrill of the challenge

There are persuasive arguments both for and against polar exploration. Logically, perhaps, it does not make sense to risk one's life travelling in such inhospitable places. However, some human beings always want to set themselves ever more difficult challenges.

And it is this – the desire to be the fastest, fittest, strongest; to climb the highest mountain; to endure the coldest temperatures on Earth – which means that new challenges will always be set. Unless international laws are passed to forbid every single person in the world from setting foot in Antarctica, there will probably always be someone who wishes to face the challenge of conquering this last, great wilderness.

THE STOLEN BACILLUS

BY H.G. WELLS

RETOLD BY BEN HULME-CROSS

ILLUSTRATED BY DANIELA TERRAZZINI

Setting the scene

A bacillus is a microscopic cell of bacteria that can cause deadly diseases. In the 1880s, scientists began using microscopes to observe these cells, discovering how the diseases spread and trying to work out how to prevent them. This story is set at that time and imagines what might happen if a bacillus got into the wrong hands.

"Would you like to see one of our most deadly diseases?" asked the Scientist, slipping a glass slide under the microscope. "These cells are a strain of the plague."

The pale young visitor peered down the microscope. "Not much to see," he said, "just little shreds of pink. Yet little cells like those could multiply – and devastate a city! Wonderful!"

As he stood up, a luminous blue cat, a subject in one of the Scientist's many experiments, crept into the room, glowing but unnoticed. "Are these cells ... alive? Are they dangerous now?" the young man continued.

"The cells you just saw have been killed; they are now completely safe," said the Scientist. "I wish, for my own part, we could kill every one of them in the universe."

"I suppose," the pale young man said with a slight smile, "that you would not dare to keep such cells in the living – in the active – state?"

"On the contrary, we must," said the Scientist, "so that we may eventually find the cure." He walked across the room and picked up one of several sealed glass tubes. "Here is the living thing. Bottled plague, so to speak."

A gleam of satisfaction appeared in the face of the pale young man. "Such a deadly thing to have in your possession," he said, his eyes fixed hungrily on the glass tube.

The pale young man had arrived at the door to the laboratory with a letter of introduction from one of the Scientist's former students. He had long, greasy, black hair and deep grey eyes. His manner was nervous, his expression haunted. He seemed a very different sort of person from anyone the Scientist knew.

I'll shake him up a bit, thought the Scientist, chuckling silently to himself. He loved an audience.

He held the tube in his hand thoughtfully. "Yes, here is the plague imprisoned. Break one little tube like this into a supply of drinking water, and havoc would soon spread through the city! Husbands taken from wives. Children taken from mothers. The plague would seek his victims everywhere. Through the pipes and sewers he would creep, bringing death in a drink ..."

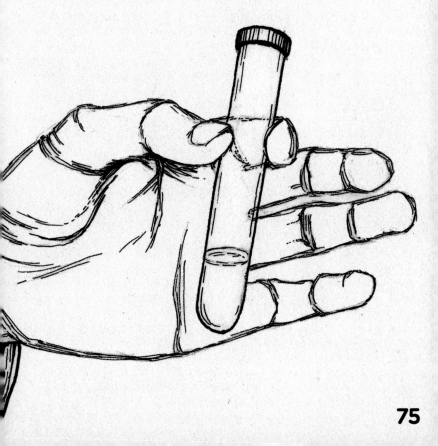

The blue cat brushed against the pale young man's leg and purred. The man felt nothing, transfixed as he was by the Scientist's description of the plague spreading through the city.

There was a knock at the door, and the Scientist placed the glass tube back with the others, then left the room for a few moments to speak with his wife.

When he re-entered the laboratory, his visitor was looking at his watch. "I had no idea I had wasted an hour of your time," the pale young man said nervously. "Your work here is very interesting, and I thank you, but now I really must go."

He hurried out of the room, repeating his thanks, and the Scientist showed him to the door before returning to his laboratory.

"He was a bit too interested in the plague," muttered the Scientist as a disturbing thought struck him.

He turned to the rack of glass tubes and noted with rising panic that one was missing. He dashed to his writing-table, felt hastily in his pockets, and then rushed to the door. "I may have put it down on the hall table," he said.

"Curses!" he shouted hoarsely in the hall. He ran out into the street and glanced wildly in both directions. The pale young man was sprinting towards the river.

"The water supply! He's mad!" groaned the Scientist. Pale and shaking, the Scientist called out to a cab that was standing idle on the corner. "To the river, man! Take me to the river!"

"Right you are, sir," said the driver, and taking note of the Scientist's expression, he cracked his whip along the horse's flank as soon as his passenger was aboard.

The Scientist sat back from his window as they overtook the pale young man. With luck he would be able to head his mad visitor off before he got to the river. The cab pulled up by the riverbank and the Scientist climbed down, tossing a few coins up to the driver.

Looking back along the street, the Scientist saw the pale young man approaching. Their eyes met and the young man froze. He reached into his coat and withdrew a glass tube.

"Please! No!" shouted the Scientist.

The pale young man raised the tube to his lips and drained it.

The Scientist fell to his knees in despair as the young man threw back his head and laughed wildly.

People passing by stopped to look at the laughing man. Stares soon became gasps. The Scientist looked up and slowly a smile of pure relief replaced his anguished expression.

The pale young man hadn't swallowed the plague. His skin was glowing a luminous blue.

Breaking
Human Limits

BY BEN HULME-CROSS

ILLUSTRATED BY SCOTT JESSOP

Setting the scene

What is the furthest you have ever run without stopping? How long can you hold your breath? Our bodies are only capable of doing so much – but is it possible for some people to do more? In this text you will find out about real people from different parts of the world, who don't seem to be limited by their bodies.

Breaking
Human Limits

Most of us have a clear idea of what is normal for a human to be able to do. Some of us can run a bit faster than others. Some can hold our breath for longer. However, most of us exist within certain limits: we need certain amounts of food, water and oxygen, we sleep within certain timeframes, and we can only do so much with those supplies.

This is true for most of us, but not all of us. Throughout the world there are people who have adapted their bodies to be able to do incredible things.

Running the distance

There are people who run huge distances as a way of life, like the Raramuri people of northern Mexico. They often run over 300 km at a time, wearing nothing but lightweight sandals called huaraches!

Where?

USA

MEXICO

Why do the Raramuri run so far?

Traditionally the Raramuri lived in small groups spread out across a huge area of mountains and canyons. To communicate with other groups they needed to travel on foot as there was no other form of transport.

DID YOU KNOW?

'Raramuri' means
'runners on foot' in
the Raramuri language.

Long-distance running is also a sport for the
Raramuri, who train from a young age by running
in groups and passing a wooden ball around
using their feet as they run. The winner is the
first to make it to the goal. These games can last
for up to two days so everyone in the community
helps the runners with water and food, lighting
the way at night and cheering them on.

Ultra-marathon runners

Many people choose to run long distances for fun! They train for months to be able to run a marathon, and most people who finish consider it to be the toughest thing they have ever done. But this isn't enough for some people – they want to take part in an ultra-marathon!

Here are some of the most popular ultra-marathons …

Ultra-trail du Mont Blanc: *in the French Alps, runners have to complete a course of around 170 km without stopping. During the race they also climb over 10 000 metres – that's higher than Mount Everest!*

DID YOU KNOW?

A normal marathon is 26 miles (42 km) long and takes place somewhere not too hot, too cold or too hilly. An ultra-marathon is any race that is longer than a normal marathon.

Jungle Ultra: *in the Amazon rainforest, runners have to cover 230 km. On the way they have to make 70 river crossings.*

DID YOU KNOW?

Every now and then a Raramuri runner will join in an ultra-marathon and annoy the other racers by making it all look very easy!

Marathon des Sables: *in the Sahara desert, runners have to cover over 250 km over six days. During the day, the temperature can exceed 50°C!*

Expert divers

The Bajau people of South East Asia live out at sea so it may not surprise you to learn that they are very good at fishing. In fact they are so good at it that many can dive down 20 metres to the seabed and hold their breath for several minutes while they hunt for fish with their spears.

MALAYSIA

INDONESIA

Where?

How have the Bajau adapted?

Incredibly, during a one-day fishing expedition, a Bajau fisherman can spend a total of five hours underwater! The Bajau people are experts at holding their breath, but studies have also shown that their eyes have adapted to see more clearly underwater than most humans do.

The Bajau often live on small houseboats just big enough for a family. When they want to spend time with other families, they meet and tie their boats together. Then when it is time to move on they can just sail away in their home. Those that live on boats usually spend much of their time tied to other boats – like little villages!

DID YOU KNOW?

The Bajau are so used to being at sea that some of them feel sick on dry land just as many people feel seasick at sea.

Free-diving

Scuba diving is a popular sport where people dive down to extreme depths with masks, wetsuits and breathing apparatus. However, some people prefer to 'free-dive' without the equipment, much like the Bajau. They can dive to depths of more than 100 metres on a single breath.

DID YOU KNOW?

Some free-divers can hold their breath for more than four minutes as they head towards the seabed.

Free-divers train over a long period to gradually increase their lung capacity, but there are risks for even the most experienced divers. The biggest risk is 'black-out' – where the diver becomes unconscious due to lack of oxygen reaching the brain. This is most common as a diver returns to the surface. Divers always have a first-aid trained 'buddy' present when practising, in case something should go wrong.

DID YOU KNOW?

Free diving is extremely dangerous and should only be attempted by professionals.

It is clear that, either by responding to the natural environment, or through determination and training, the human body can achieve great things. What other amazing adaptations are humans capable of?

How have people living at high altitudes such as the Andes Mountains adapted over time?

What kind of training do jet pilots need to undertake to deal with the extreme gravitational forces of high-speed flight?

What adaptations do you think humans might make in the future?

THE TUESDAY THING

BY BEN HULME-CROSS
ILLUSTRATED BY EUAN COOK

Setting the scene

Sometimes extraordinary things happen in
ordinary places to ordinary people. These
mysterious events seem impossible to
understand or explain. This story is one of
those mysteries ... Read on and see if *you*
can work out what has happened.

It was the weirdest thing ever. The Tuesday thing, we call it. Jake and me and my little brother Noah were playing football in the park. It was nearly winter and nearly dark and nearly time to go home. And it was Tuesday and we had school the next day and Mum made me promise to come home as soon as Noah got tired. And it was windy and cold and there were bits of sleet in the air.

"Tommy!" says Noah. "I wanna go home." But you can't let them have their way all the time, so I kick the ball as hard as I can and it flies up over the goal and into a little patch of trees.

"All right," I say. "Get the ball and we'll go home." Jake laughs and Noah pulls a face but he walks off towards the trees anyway. Noah's not bad, for a little brother. He knows who's boss when I'm with my mates.

Then Jake and me are messing around by the goal seeing who can get closest to the crossbar when we jump. Jake's taller than me but I'm lighter and I'm winning easily. Then I land weirdly and I'm all off-balance and I sort of trip backwards and smack into one of the goalposts. I'm sitting on the ground, winded, and Jake's laughing his head off. That makes me angry and I'm about to get up and give Jake a shove when we see that Noah's back.

"Guys ..." his voice sounds all small and strange even though he's standing right there, and something about his face makes me forget about Jake laughing.

"What is it?"

Noah just swallows and points at the trees and then he starts walking over there again so, of course, me and Jake go with him. There's a low wooden rail around the trees and a litter bin and a sign saying 'PICK IT UP!' and we've been there a hundred times before but never like this. Noah steps over the wooden rail and we follow him into the trees until he just stops.

At first we can't see anything but then Noah moves to the side and he's pointing down at the ground and there, all crouched down and holding our football out in front of him, is a boy about our age.

Jake's got a torch with him and he switches
it on and shines it at the kid on the ground and
he doesn't even blink, just stares right at us. And
we know straight away there's something wrong.
He's got this mark like a tattoo right in the
middle of his forehead – lots of black dots in a
swirl like a snail-shell.

"What are you doing?" says Jake. "Are you gonna give us our ball back or what?"

And the kid doesn't say anything but he puts the ball on the ground and it rolls over towards Jake, even though he doesn't push the ball to make it roll and there isn't a slope.

"Tommy!" says Noah. "I wanna go home."

And Jake says, "Yeah, let's go."

And there's something scary in the air, we can all feel it. But I just want to know what's happening, so I say "Wait!" And then I'm asking the kid all these questions like about the mark on his head and where he's from and what team does he support, and he just crouches there, staring up at us while Jake shines the light in his face. And then I think maybe he's not staring *at* us, maybe he's staring *through* us and I get the shivers and I'm about to say, "Let's go" when the kid stands up all of a sudden. And the three of us get a bit of a fright and the kid just starts walking and we get out of his way.

When he's close he's staring straight ahead and Jake's still got the torch on his face, and the dots on his forehead look like they're moving – like they're spinning round in tiny circles. I blink and shake my head, *they can't be*, and he's passed us. He steps over the rail and he walks out into the middle of the football pitch.

We all want to run away but we all want to stay and find out more about the kid, so we follow him but we keep our distance as well. Jake's got the torch on the kid the whole time. And what happens ... well, me and Jake and Noah talk about it sometimes but we've never told anyone else. They'd lock us up. We know it's true, though, because the torch stays on the whole time. We've got it trained on the kid, so we can see exactly where he goes and what he does.

All of a sudden the kid looks straight up. And there's this weird feeling in the air, like just before thunder when it feels like everything gets heavier, and we're looking right at the kid and the dots have started glowing green. And we can't take our eyes off him. We're all three of us staring right at him, lit up by the torch. The thunder feeling gets stronger and stronger.

And then the kid's just not there any more.